how

to

pleasure

your

woman

during

s

e

x

CW00349774

Chapter 1: Understanding Female Anatom

Introduction to the female reproductive s

Key erogenous zones and pleasure points

Understanding the clitoris, G-spot, and other sensitive areas

Chapter 2: Communication and Consent

Importance of open communication with your partner

Discussing desires, boundaries, and preferences

The role of consent in pleasurable experiences

Chapter 3: Foreplay Techniques

Importance of foreplay in female arousal

Various foreplay techniques such as kissing, caressing, and massaging

Tips for exploring different erogenous zones

Chapter 4: Oral Sex Mastery

Guide to performing cunnilingus

Techniques for stimulating the clitoris and surrounding areas

Communication and feedback during oral sex

Chapter 5: Manual Stimulation

Exploring techniques for manual stimulation of the clitoris and G-spot

Using fingers and hands to enhance pleasure

Incorporating different rhythms and pressures

Chapter 6: Positions for Maximum Pleasure

Overview of sex positions that provide optimal stimulation for women

Tips for finding the right angles and depths

Incorporating variety and experimentation into your sex life

Chapter 7: The Role of Sensory Stimulation

Incorporating sensory play into sexual experiences

Using props, toys, and accessories to enhance pleasure

Exploring the connection between sensory stimulation and arousal

Chapter 8: Emotional Connection and Intimacy

Importance of emotional connection in sexual pleasure

Building intimacy through communication and trust

Techniques for deepening emotional connection during sex

Chapter 1: Understanding Female Anatomy

1.1 Introduction to the Female Reproductive System

The female reproductive system is a complex and intricate network of organs and structures designed to produce offspring. Understanding the basics of this system is crucial for both women and their partners to appreciate the nuances of sexual pleasure and reproductive health.

Anatomy of the Female Reproductive System

The primary organs of the female reproductive system include:

Ovaries: Two small, almond-shaped organs located on either side of the uterus. Ovaries produce eggs (ova) and hormones such as estrogen and progesterone.

Fallopian Tubes: Narrow tubes that connect the ovaries to the uterus. Fertilization of an egg typically occurs within the fallopian tubes.

Uterus (Womb): A pear-shaped organ where a fertilized egg implants and grows during pregnancy.

Cervix: The lower part of the uterus that connects to the vagina. The cervix secretes mucus that changes in consistency throughout the menstrual cycle.

Vagina: A muscular canal that extends from the cervix to the external genitalia. The vagina serves as the birth canal during childbirth and facilitates sexual intercourse.

Menstrual Cycle

The menstrual cycle is a monthly series of hormonal changes that prepares the female body for pregnancy.

Key phases of the menstrual cycle include:

Menstruation: Shedding of the uterine lining, typically lasting 3-7 days.

Follicular Phase: Development of ovarian follicles and a rise in estrogen levels.

Ovulation: Release of a mature egg from an ovarian follicle, typically around mid-cycle.

Luteal Phase: Formation of the corpus luteum and a surge in progesterone levels to prepare the uterus for potential implantation.

Hormonal Regulation

Hormones play a critical role in regulating the female reproductive system.

Key hormones involved include:

Estrogen: Primarily produced by the ovaries, estrogen influences the development of secondary sexual characteristics and helps regulate the menstrual cycle.

Progesterone: Produced by the corpus luteum, progesterone prepares the uterus for implantation and supports early pregnancy.

Follicle-Stimulating Hormone (FSH) and Luteinizing Hormone (LH): Produced by the pituitary gland, FSH and LH stimulate follicle development, ovulation, and hormone production in the ovaries.

Understanding the anatomy and physiology of the female reproductive system lays the foundation for exploring topics related to sexual pleasure, fertility, and reproductive health. In the following chapters, we will delve deeper into specific aspects of female sexual anatomy and techniques for enhancing pleasure and intimacy.

1.2 Key Erogenous Zones and Pleasure Points

Understanding the various erogenous zones and pleasure points on a woman's body is essential for unlocking new levels of sexual pleasure and intimacy. By exploring and stimulating these sensitive areas, partners can enhance arousal and create deeply satisfying experiences. In this chapter, we'll explore some of the primary erogenous zones and techniques for pleasuring them.

The Clitoris: The Queen of Erogenous Zones

The clitoris is often considered the most sensitive erogenous zone on a woman's body.

Located at the top of the vulva, just above the vaginal opening, the clitoris contains thousands of nerve endings.

Techniques for stimulating the clitoris include:

Gentle circular motions with fingers or tongue.

Light sucking or nibbling.

Using lubrication to enhance sensation.

Experimenting with different pressure and speed.

mmunication is key – ask your partner what feels best and adjust your technique cordingly.

e G-Spot: A Source of Intense Pleasure

e G-spot is an area of heightened sensitivity located inside the vagina, typically about 1-2 ches along the front vaginal wall.

imulation of the G-spot can lead to intense orgasms and even female ejaculation for some omen.

chniques for G-spot stimulation include:

sing fingers with a "come hither" motion to apply pressure to the front vaginal wall.

perimenting with different angles and depths of penetration.

corporating toys designed for G-spot stimulation, such as curved dildos or vibrators.

tience and exploration are key – the G-spot may vary in size and sensitivity among dividuals.

ipples and Breast Stimulation

ne nipples and breasts are highly sensitive areas for many women and can be potent ources of arousal.

chniques for stimulating the nipples and breasts include:

ght touching, licking, and sucking.

perimenting with different pressures and speeds.

corporating temperature play by using ice cubes or warm breath.

ommunicating with your partner to gauge their preferences and comfort levels.

emember to pay attention to non-verbal cues and adjust your technique accordingly.

ther Erogenous Zones to Explore

addition to the clitoris, G-spot, nipples, and breasts, there are numerous other erogenous ones on a woman's body worth exploring.

nese may include:

ne inner thighs: Gentle kisses or caresses can build anticipation and arousal.

ne neck and ears: Light kisses, nibbles, and whispered words can be incredibly arousing.

The lower back and buttocks: Massage and gentle pressure can stimulate nerve endings and enhance arousal.

Every woman is unique, so take the time to discover and prioritize your partner's individual pleasure points.

By exploring and pleasuring these key erogenous zones, partners can deepen their connection, enhance arousal, and create more fulfilling sexual experiences. In the following chapters, we'll delve into specific techniques and strategies for maximizing pleasure and intimacy in the bedroom.

1.3 Understanding the Clitoris, G-spot, and Other Sensitive Areas

In this chapter, we will delve into the anatomy and intricacies of the clitoris, G-spot, and other sensitive areas of a woman's body. Understanding these key pleasure points is essential for unlocking the full potential of sexual pleasure and intimacy.

The Clitoris: The Epicenter of Female Pleasure

The clitoris is a small, highly sensitive organ located at the top of the vulva, beneath the clitoral hood.

Despite its small size, the clitoris contains thousands of nerve endings, making it extremely sensitive to touch.

The clitoris is often considered the primary source of female sexual pleasure and is crucial for achieving orgasm.

Techniques for stimulating the clitoris include:

Using fingers or the tongue to gently rub or circle the clitoral hood.

Applying varying degrees of pressure and speed to explore different sensations.

Incorporating sex toys such as vibrators designed for clitoral stimulation.

Communication is key – encourage your partner to provide feedback on what feels most pleasurable.

The G-spot: A Source of Deep Pleasure and Intense Orgasms

The G-spot is an area of heightened sensitivity located inside the vagina, typically about 1-. inches along the front vaginal wall.

Stimulation of the G-spot can lead to intense sensations and even squirting orgasms for some women.

While the existence and location of the G-spot may vary among individuals, many women report heightened pleasure when this area is stimulated.

Techniques for stimulating the G-spot include:

Using a "come hither" motion with the fingers to apply pressure to the front wall of the vagina.

Experimenting with different angles and depths of penetration to target the G-spot.

Trying specialized G-spot vibrators or curved toys for enhanced stimulation.

Patience and exploration are key – every woman's G-spot sensitivity and responsiveness may vary.

Other Sensitive Areas to Explore

In addition to the clitoris and G-spot, there are numerous other sensitive areas on a woman's body that can elicit pleasure and arousal.

These may include:

The inner thighs: Gentle kisses, nibbles, or soft strokes can build anticipation and arousal.

The nipples and breasts: Light caresses, kisses, and gentle stimulation can be highly arousing for many women.

The neck, ears, and lips: Whispered words, kisses, and gentle nibbles can heighten arousal and intimacy.

Take the time to explore and prioritize your partner's unique pleasure points, and pay attention to verbal and non-verbal cues.

Understanding the clitoris, G-spot, and other sensitive areas of a woman's body is essential for enhancing sexual pleasure and intimacy. In the following chapters, we will delve into specific techniques and strategies for pleasuring these areas and creating deeply satisfying sexual experiences.

Chapter 2: Communication and Consent

2.1 Importance of Open Communication with Your Partner

Effective communication is the cornerstone of a healthy and fulfilling sexual relationship. In this chapter, we'll explore the significance of open communication with your partner and how it can enhance intimacy, pleasure, and overall satisfaction.

Building Trust and Connection

Open communication fosters trust and connection between partners, creating a safe space to express desires, concerns, and boundaries.

By openly discussing sexual preferences, fantasies, and concerns, partners can deepen their understanding of each other's needs and desires.

Enhancing Sexual Pleasure

Communicating openly about likes, dislikes, and preferences allows partners to tailor their sexual experiences to each other's pleasure.

Sharing feedback during sexual encounters helps partners understand what feels good and what could be improved, leading to more satisfying experiences for both parties.

Addressing Concerns and Resolving Issues

Open communication enables partners to address concerns or issues that may arise in the bedroom, such as performance anxiety, discomfort, or insecurities.

By openly discussing these concerns, partners can work together to find solutions and strengthen their connection.

Setting and Respecting Boundaries

Open communication empowers partners to establish and respect boundaries, ensuring that both parties feel safe and comfortable during sexual interactions.

Discussing boundaries, such as consent, sexual activities, and limits, helps build mutual respect and trust within the relationship.

Nurturing Emotional Intimacy

Open communication fosters emotional intimacy by allowing partners to share their vulnerabilities, desires, and feelings with each other.

Talking openly about sexual desires, fantasies, and emotions deepens the emotional connection between partners and strengthens the bond in the relationship.

Tips for Effective Communication

Create a safe and non-judgmental environment where both partners feel comfortable expressing themselves openly.

Practice active listening by paying attention to your partner's verbal and non-verbal cues and responding with empathy and understanding.

Be honest and transparent about your own feelings, desires, and boundaries, and encourage your partner to do the same.

Use "I" statements to express your thoughts and feelings without blaming or criticizing your partner.

Regularly check in with your partner outside of sexual encounters to discuss any concerns, desires, or changes in preferences.

By prioritizing open communication with your partner, you can deepen your connection, enhance sexual pleasure, and cultivate a more fulfilling and satisfying relationship. In the following chapters, we'll explore specific techniques and strategies for improving communication in the bedroom and maximizing pleasure together.

2.2 Discussing Desires, Boundaries, and Preferences

Openly discussing desires, boundaries, and preferences with your partner is crucial for building trust, enhancing intimacy, and creating mutually satisfying sexual experiences. In this chapter, we'll explore the importance of having these conversations and provide guidance on how to approach them.

Importance of Discussing Desires

Sharing your sexual desires with your partner can lead to greater satisfaction and fulfillment in your relationship.

Discussing desires allows both partners to understand each other's wants and needs, fostering a deeper connection and sense of intimacy.

Exploring fantasies and desires together can add excitement and novelty to your sexual experiences.

Setting Boundaries and Respecting Limits

Establishing boundaries is essential for ensuring that both partners feel safe and comfortable during sexual interactions.

Discussing boundaries helps clarify expectations and ensures that both partners are on the same page regarding what is acceptable and what is not.

Respecting your partner's boundaries is crucial for maintaining trust and mutual respect within the relationship.

Communicating Preferences and Likes

Sharing preferences and likes allows partners to learn what brings pleasure to each other and how to best satisfy each other's needs.

Discussing preferences can lead to more enjoyable and fulfilling sexual encounters by focusing on activities and techniques that both partners enjoy.

Regularly checking in with each other about preferences ensures that both partners feel heard and valued in the relationship.

Approaching the Conversation

Choose an appropriate time and place to have the conversation, ensuring privacy and minimizing distractions.

Start the conversation by expressing your own desires, boundaries, and preferences openly and honestly.

Encourage your partner to share their thoughts and feelings without judgment or criticism.

Use active listening techniques to ensure that both partners feel heard and understood.

Be respectful and empathetic towards your partner's feelings and needs, even if they differ from your own.

Reassure your partner that discussing desires and boundaries is a normal and healthy part of any relationship.

Building Trust and Intimacy

ngaging in open and honest conversations about desires, boundaries, and preferences
rengthens trust and intimacy between partners.

aring vulnerabilities and insecurities fosters a deeper emotional connection and
rengthens the bond in the relationship.

ntinuously communicating and checking in with each other builds a strong foundation of
ust and understanding, enhancing the overall quality of the relationship.

discussing desires, boundaries, and preferences openly and honestly, partners can
epen their connection, enhance intimacy, and create more satisfying sexual experiences
gether. In the following chapters, we'll explore specific techniques and strategies for
plementing these conversations and maximizing pleasure in the bedroom.

3 The Role of Consent in Pleasurable Experiences

nsent is the cornerstone of healthy and enjoyable sexual experiences. In this chapter,
e'll explore the importance of consent, how to establish it, and why it's essential for
eating mutually satisfying encounters.

nderstanding Consent

nsent is the enthusiastic, informed, and voluntary agreement to engage in sexual activity.

is an ongoing process that requires clear communication and mutual understanding
etween all parties involved.

nsent must be freely given and can be revoked at any time.

portance of Consent in Pleasure

nsent ensures that all parties involved are comfortable, respected, and able to fully enjoy
e sexual experience.

hen both partners enthusiastically consent to sexual activity, it creates a sense of trust,
fety, and mutual respect, enhancing pleasure for everyone involved.

espect for boundaries and desires is fundamental to creating an environment where
easure can flourish.

Establishing Consent

Communicate openly and honestly with your partner about your desires, boundaries, and intentions.

Ask for consent before initiating any sexual activity, and listen carefully to your partner's response.

Pay attention to verbal and non-verbal cues to ensure that your partner is comfortable and enthusiastic about the encounter.

Respect your partner's boundaries and preferences, and be prepared to adjust your actions accordingly.

Consent and Non-Verbal Communication

Non-verbal cues such as body language, facial expressions, and vocal tone can convey important information about consent.

Pay attention to your partner's reactions and responses throughout the sexual encounter, and be prepared to pause or stop if you sense any hesitation or discomfort.

Remember that silence or lack of resistance does not imply consent – it's essential to explicitly seek and obtain verbal confirmation.

Consent and Intoxication

Consent cannot be given if a person is intoxicated or otherwise incapacitated.

It is never okay to engage in sexual activity with someone who is unable to give clear and coherent consent.

If you or your partner have been drinking or using drugs, it's crucial to wait until both parties are sober before initiating sexual activity.

Affirmative Consent

Affirmative consent is an enthusiastic and explicit agreement to engage in sexual activity.

It involves actively seeking and receiving a clear "yes" from your partner before proceeding with any sexual activity.

Affirmative consent ensures that all parties are fully aware of and enthusiastic about the sexual encounter, leading to more pleasurable and fulfilling experiences.

By prioritizing consent in sexual encounters, partners can create a safe, respectful, and pleasurable environment where all parties feel valued and respected. In the following chapters, we'll explore specific techniques and strategies for enhancing pleasure while prioritizing consent and respect.

Chapter 3: Foreplay Techniques

3.1 The Importance of Foreplay in Female Arousal

Foreplay plays a crucial role in enhancing female arousal, pleasure, and overall sexual satisfaction. In this chapter, we'll delve into why foreplay is essential, its benefits, and techniques for incorporating it into your sexual experiences.

Understanding Foreplay

Foreplay refers to the various sexual activities that occur before penetrative intercourse, including kissing, touching, oral sex, and mutual exploration of erogenous zones.

It serves as a vital precursor to intercourse, preparing the body and mind for heightened arousal and pleasure.

Foreplay allows partners to connect emotionally and physically, building anticipation and excitement for the sexual encounter.

Stimulating Arousal

Foreplay is instrumental in stimulating arousal and increasing blood flow to the genital area, making penetrative sex more enjoyable and comfortable for both partners.

It helps relax the body and mind, reducing anxiety and tension, which can inhibit sexual response.

By focusing on pleasurable sensations and building anticipation, foreplay sets the stage for more intense and satisfying orgasms.

Enhancing Lubrication

Foreplay encourages the body to produce natural lubrication, reducing friction and discomfort during intercourse.

Adequate lubrication is essential for preventing vaginal dryness and discomfort, enhancing pleasure and minimizing the risk of irritation or injury.

Exploring Sensuality and Intimacy

Foreplay allows partners to explore each other's bodies and discover what feels pleasurable and arousing.

It fosters intimacy and emotional connection, deepening the bond between partners and creating a more fulfilling sexual experience.

By taking the time to focus on each other's needs and desires, foreplay builds trust, communication, and mutual satisfaction.

Techniques for Foreplay

Experiment with a variety of techniques and activities, including kissing, caressing, massaging, and oral sex.

Pay attention to your partner's responses and cues, adjusting your technique to maximize pleasure and arousal.

Incorporate sensory stimulation, such as using feathers, ice cubes, or scented oils, to heighten sensation and arousal.

Take your time and savor each moment, focusing on building anticipation and intimacy before moving on to penetrative sex.

Communicating During Foreplay

Communication is key during foreplay, allowing partners to express their desires, boundaries, and preferences.

Encourage open dialogue about what feels good and what doesn't, and be receptive to your partner's feedback and cues.

Check in with each other regularly to ensure that both partners are comfortable and enjoying the experience.

By prioritizing foreplay in your sexual encounters, you can enhance arousal, pleasure, and intimacy, leading to more satisfying and fulfilling experiences for both partners. In the following chapters, we'll explore specific techniques and strategies for incorporating foreplay into your sexual repertoire and maximizing pleasure in the bedroom.

3.2 Exploring Foreplay Techniques: Kissing, Caressing, and Massaging

Foreplay is a vital aspect of sexual intimacy, providing an opportunity to build arousal, anticipation, and connection between partners. In this chapter, we'll explore various foreplay techniques, including kissing, caressing, and massaging, and how they can enhance pleasure and intimacy.

The Art of Kissing

Kissing is one of the most intimate and sensual forms of foreplay, stimulating the lips, tongue, and mouth, which are rich in nerve endings.

Techniques for kissing include:

Soft, gentle kisses on the lips to build anticipation.

Deep, passionate kisses to ignite arousal and desire.

Nibbling or sucking on the lips and exploring your partner's mouth with your tongue.

Experiment with different kissing styles and rhythms to discover what feels most pleasurable for you and your partner.

Sensual Caressing

Caressing involves gently touching and stroking your partner's body to create sensations of pleasure and arousal.

Techniques for caressing include:

Using your fingertips to trace light patterns on your partner's skin.

Running your hands through your partner's hair or gently massaging their scalp.

Exploring different textures, such as silk or feathers, to enhance sensory stimulation.

Pay attention to your partner's responses and adjust your touch to match their preferences and comfort level.

Therapeutic Massage

Massage is a deeply relaxing and intimate form of foreplay that can help release tension, reduce stress, and enhance arousal.

Techniques for massage include:

Using long, flowing strokes to warm up the muscles and relax the body.

pplying gentle pressure to key areas, such as the shoulders, neck, and lower back, to
elease tension.

ncorporating sensual touches, such as kneading or circular motions, to stimulate erogenous
ones and increase arousal.

xperiment with different massage oils or lotions to enhance glide and sensory stimulation.

ncorporating Foreplay into Your Routine

oreplay doesn't have to be limited to the bedroom – it can occur at any time and in any
ocation.

ake advantage of opportunities throughout the day to engage in playful touches, flirtatious
estures, and whispered words of desire.

et aside dedicated time for foreplay during sexual encounters, allowing you and your
artner to fully immerse yourselves in the experience and build anticipation.

ommunication and Feedback

ommunication is essential during foreplay, allowing partners to express their desires,
oundaries, and preferences.

ncourage open dialogue about what feels good and what doesn't, and be receptive to your
artner's feedback and cues.

heck in with each other regularly to ensure that both partners are comfortable and
njoying the experience.

y incorporating kissing, caressing, and massaging into your foreplay routine, you can
nhance arousal, pleasure, and intimacy with your partner, leading to more satisfying and
ulfilling sexual experiences. In the following chapters, we'll explore additional foreplay
echniques and strategies for maximizing pleasure in the bedroom.

.3 Tips for Exploring Different Erogenous Zones

rogenous zones are areas of the body that are particularly sensitive to touch and can elicit
leasurable sensations when stimulated. In this chapter, we'll explore tips for exploring and
leasuring various erogenous zones, enhancing arousal and intimacy between partners.

Understanding Erogenous Zones

Erogenous zones vary from person to person but commonly include areas such as the lips, neck, ears, nipples, inner thighs, and genitals.

Exploring and stimulating these zones can enhance arousal, increase blood flow to the genital area, and build anticipation for sexual activity.

Start Slow and Build Anticipation

Begin by gently touching and caressing your partner's body, focusing on areas that are known to be erogenous zones.

Use light, teasing touches to build anticipation and heighten arousal before moving on to more intense stimulation.

Pay Attention to Non-Verbal Cues

Pay close attention to your partner's reactions and responses as you explore different erogenous zones.

Look for signs of pleasure, such as moans, sighs, or changes in breathing, and adjust your technique accordingly.

Communicate and Ask for Feedback

Encourage open communication with your partner about what feels pleasurable and what doesn't.

Ask for feedback and guidance as you explore different erogenous zones, and be receptive to your partner's cues and preferences.

Incorporate Variety and Creativity

Experiment with different techniques and sensations to stimulate erogenous zones, such as kissing, licking, sucking, nibbling, and gentle scratching.

Try using different textures, temperatures, and sensations, such as feathers, ice cubes, or silk scarves, to enhance arousal and pleasure.

Focus on the Entire Body

While certain areas may be more sensitive than others, don't neglect other parts of the body during foreplay.

Explore areas such as the back, shoulders, arms, and feet, using gentle touches and massages to relax and arouse your partner.

Use Lubrication

When stimulating erogenous zones such as the genitals, consider using a water-based lubricant to enhance glide and reduce friction.

Lubrication can increase comfort and pleasure, allowing for more intense and enjoyable sensations.

Be Patient and Take Your Time

Don't rush through the process of exploring erogenous zones – take your time and savor each moment.

Focus on building anticipation and connection with your partner, allowing arousal to build gradually before moving on to more intimate activities.

By taking the time to explore and pleasure different erogenous zones, you can enhance arousal, intimacy, and overall sexual satisfaction with your partner. In the following chapters, we'll continue to explore techniques and strategies for maximizing pleasure and connection in the bedroom.

Chapter 4: Oral Sex Mastery

4.1 Guide to Performing Cunnilingus

Cunnilingus, or oral sex performed on a woman's genitals, can be an incredibly pleasurable and intimate experience when done with care and attention. In this chapter, we'll explore a guide to performing cunnilingus, including techniques, tips, and considerations for maximizing pleasure for both partners.

Creating a Comfortable Environment

Ensure that both you and your partner are comfortable and relaxed before engaging in cunnilingus.

Choose a comfortable position for both partners, such as lying down with the receiving partner's legs spread or elevated.

Communication and Consent

Prioritize open communication with your partner about their desires, boundaries, and preferences regarding cunnilingus.

Obtain enthusiastic consent before initiating oral sex, and continuously check in with your partner throughout the experience.

Technique and Approach

Begin by gently kissing and caressing your partner's thighs and pelvic area to build anticipation.

Use your tongue to explore the entire vulva, including the labia, clitoral hood, and vaginal opening.

Experiment with different techniques, such as licking, sucking, and gently nibbling, to vary sensation and intensity.

Pay attention to your partner's verbal and non-verbal cues to gauge what feels pleasurable and adjust your technique accordingly.

Focus on the Clitoris

The clitoris is often the most sensitive part of the vulva and a primary source of pleasure for many women.

Use your tongue to gently stimulate the clitoral hood and shaft, experimenting with different rhythms, pressures, and speeds.

Communicate with your partner to determine the level of direct clitoral stimulation that feels most pleasurable.

Incorporate Variation and Creativity

Explore different areas of the vulva, including the inner and outer labia, perineum, and vaginal opening, to provide varied sensations.

Experiment with using your fingers or a sex toy, such as a vibrator, to complement oral stimulation and enhance pleasure.

Maintain Hygiene and Safety

Ensure that your mouth and hands are clean before engaging in cunnilingus to reduce the risk of infection.

Consider using a dental dam or plastic wrap as a barrier to protect against sexually transmitted infections (STIs), especially if you or your partner have multiple partners or are at risk for STIs.

Take Your Time and Enjoy the Experience

Cunnilingus is not a race – take your time to explore and pleasure your partner's body, savoring each moment.

Focus on creating a connection with your partner and enjoying the intimate experience together.

By following this guide to performing cunnilingus and prioritizing your partner's pleasure and comfort, you can create deeply satisfying and intimate experiences in the bedroom. In the following chapters, we'll continue to explore techniques and strategies for enhancing pleasure and connection during sexual encounters.

4.2 Techniques for Stimulating the Clitoris and Surrounding Areas

The clitoris and its surrounding areas are highly sensitive and can be a source of intense pleasure for many women. In this chapter, we'll explore techniques for stimulating the clitoris and its surrounding areas to enhance arousal and pleasure during sexual encounters.

Understanding the Clitoris and Surrounding Areas

The clitoris is a small, highly sensitive organ located at the top of the vulva, beneath the clitoral hood.

Surrounding areas include the clitoral hood, labia minora, and vestibular bulbs, all of which can contribute to pleasurable sensations when stimulated.

Techniques for Clitoral Stimulation

Use your fingers or tongue to gently stimulate the clitoris through the clitoral hood.

Experiment with different rhythms, pressures, and speeds to find what feels most pleasurable for your partner.

Try using circular motions, up-and-down movements, or side-to-side strokes to vary sensation and intensity.

Incorporating the Clitoral Hood

The clitoral hood is a fold of skin that covers and protects the clitoris.

Gently massage and caress the clitoral hood to stimulate the clitoris indirectly and build anticipation.

Use your tongue to flick or tease the clitoral hood, alternating between light and firmer pressure.

Exploring the Labia Minora

The labia minora are the inner folds of skin surrounding the vaginal opening.

Use your fingers or tongue to trace gentle circles or strokes along the length of the labia minora, paying attention to your partner's responses.

Experiment with gently pulling or tugging on the labia minora to vary sensation and increase arousal.

Stimulating the Vestibular Bulbs

he vestibular bulbs are erectile tissues located on either side of the vaginal opening.

se your fingers or tongue to massage and stimulate the vestibular bulbs, applying gentle ressure and rhythmic movements.

xperiment with incorporating light tapping or squeezing motions to increase blood flow nd arousal in this area.

ombination Techniques

ombine clitoral stimulation with stimulation of other erogenous zones, such as the nipples, ner thighs, or G-spot, to enhance pleasure and arousal.

se your fingers, tongue, and even sex toys to explore and stimulate multiple areas multaneously.

ommunication and Feedback

ncourage open communication with your partner about what feels pleasurable and what oesn't.

ay attention to your partner's verbal and non-verbal cues to gauge their level of arousal nd adjust your technique accordingly.

y incorporating these techniques for stimulating the clitoris and surrounding areas into our sexual encounters, you can enhance arousal, pleasure, and intimacy with your partner. the following chapters, we'll continue to explore techniques and strategies for maximizing leasure and connection in the bedroom.

.3 Communication and Feedback During Oral Sex

ffective communication and feedback are essential elements of a satisfying oral sex xperience. In this chapter, we'll explore the importance of communication, how to give and ceive feedback during oral sex, and tips for enhancing pleasure and connection between artners.

nportance of Communication

ommunication during oral sex helps partners understand each other's desires, preferences, nd boundaries.

It creates a safe and comfortable environment where partners can express their needs and explore new sensations.

Open communication fosters trust, intimacy, and mutual satisfaction in the sexual relationship.

Giving Feedback

Encourage your partner to communicate what feels pleasurable and what doesn't during oral sex.

Provide positive reinforcement for techniques or movements that feel good, such as moans sighs, or verbal encouragement.

Use gentle guidance and encouragement to communicate any adjustments or changes you like your partner to make.

Receiving Feedback

Be receptive to feedback from your partner during oral sex, and avoid taking constructive criticism personally.

Pay attention to your partner's verbal and non-verbal cues to gauge their level of arousal and adjust your technique accordingly.

Ask for specific feedback if you're unsure about what your partner enjoys or prefers, and be open to trying new techniques.

Non-Verbal Communication

Non-verbal cues, such as moans, sighs, and body movements, can convey important information about your partner's level of arousal and pleasure.

Pay attention to your partner's reactions and respond accordingly, adjusting your technique to maximize pleasure.

Use your own body language to express enthusiasm and enjoyment, reinforcing a positive and intimate connection with your partner.

Creating a Safe and Comfortable Environment

Prioritize creating a safe and comfortable environment for communication during oral sex.

Choose a quiet and private setting where you and your partner feel relaxed and free from distractions.

Encourage open dialogue and reassure your partner that their feedback is valued and respected.

Using Positive Reinforcement

Offer positive reinforcement to your partner during oral sex, acknowledging and appreciating their efforts to pleasure you.

Verbalize your pleasure and gratitude for their attentiveness and skill, reinforcing a sense of mutual satisfaction and connection.

Practice Active Listening

Practice active listening during oral sex, paying attention to your partner's verbal and non-verbal cues and responding with empathy and understanding.

Show genuine interest in your partner's pleasure and satisfaction, and be responsive to their needs and desires.

By prioritizing communication and feedback during oral sex, partners can enhance arousal, pleasure, and intimacy, creating deeply satisfying sexual experiences together. In the following chapters, we'll continue to explore techniques and strategies for maximizing pleasure and connection in the bedroom.

Chapter 5: Manual Stimulation

5.1 Exploring Techniques for Manual Stimulation of the Clitoris and G-spot

Manual stimulation of the clitoris and G-spot can be incredibly pleasurable and intimate for both partners. In this chapter, we'll explore techniques for stimulating these erogenous zones manually, enhancing arousal and pleasure during sexual encounters.

Understanding the Clitoris and G-spot

The clitoris is a small, highly sensitive organ located at the top of the vulva, beneath the clitoral hood, and is a primary source of pleasure for many women.

The G-spot is an area of heightened sensitivity located inside the vagina, typically about 1-2 inches along the front vaginal wall, and can yield intense sensations and orgasms for some women.

Techniques for Clitoral Stimulation

Use your fingers to gently massage and stimulate the clitoris through the clitoral hood.

Experiment with different rhythms, pressures, and speeds to find what feels most pleasurable for your partner.

Try using circular motions, up-and-down movements, or side-to-side strokes to vary sensation and intensity.

Incorporating the G-spot

Use one or two fingers to explore the front wall of the vagina, about 1-2 inches inside, to locate the G-spot.

Apply firm pressure to the G-spot and experiment with a "come hither" motion to stimulate the area.

Communicate with your partner to determine the level of pressure and sensation that feels most pleasurable.

Combination Techniques

Combine clitoral and G-spot stimulation for a more intense and pleasurable experience.

Use your fingers to stimulate the clitoris while simultaneously applying pressure to the G-spot, or vice versa, to create dual sensations and increase arousal.

Using Lubrication

Consider using a water-based lubricant to enhance glide and reduce friction during manual stimulation.

Lubrication can increase comfort and pleasure, allowing for smoother and more enjoyable sensations.

Paying Attention to Feedback

Encourage your partner to provide feedback during manual stimulation, communicating what feels pleasurable and what doesn't.

Pay attention to your partner's verbal and non-verbal cues to gauge their level of arousal and adjust your technique accordingly.

Exploring Different Positions

Experiment with different positions for manual stimulation, such as lying down, sitting up, or kneeling between your partner's legs.

Find a position that allows for comfortable access to the clitoris and G-spot and allows both partners to relax and enjoy the experience.

Taking Your Time and Enjoying the Experience

Manual stimulation is not a race – take your time to explore and pleasure your partner's body, savoring each moment.

Focus on creating a connection with your partner and enjoying the intimate experience together.

5.2 Using Fingers and Hands to Enhance Pleasure

Fingers and hands can be powerful tools for enhancing pleasure and intimacy during sexual encounters. In this chapter, we'll explore various techniques for using fingers and hands to stimulate erogenous zones and create deeply satisfying experiences for both partners.

Understanding the Power of Touch

Touch is a fundamental aspect of human sexuality and can convey intimacy, arousal, and pleasure.

Fingers and hands are versatile tools for exploring and stimulating erogenous zones, enhancing arousal and pleasure during sexual encounters.

Techniques for Using Fingers and Hands

Experiment with different techniques for using fingers and hands to stimulate erogenous zones, including the clitoris, G-spot, nipples, and other sensitive areas.

Use gentle, caressing touches to build anticipation and arousal, gradually increasing pressure and intensity as desired.

Explore different rhythms, speeds, and movements, such as circular motions, tapping, or gentle squeezing, to vary sensation and increase pleasure.

Clitoral Stimulation

Use your fingers to stimulate the clitoris, applying gentle pressure and varying strokes to explore what feels pleasurable for your partner.

Experiment with using one finger, multiple fingers, or the palm of your hand to provide different sensations and intensities of stimulation.

Communicate with your partner to determine the level of pressure and sensation that feels most pleasurable.

G-spot Stimulation

Use a "come hither" motion with your fingers to stimulate the G-spot, applying firm pressure to the front wall of the vagina.

Experiment with different angles and depths of penetration to target the G-spot and explore what feels most pleasurable for your partner.

Consider using a curved or textured toy to enhance G-spot stimulation and increase arousal.

Nipple Stimulation

e your fingers and hands to gently massage and caress the nipples, paying attention to ur partner's responses and adjusting your technique accordingly.

periment with different levels of pressure and sensation, such as light tapping, circular otions, or gentle pinching, to enhance arousal and pleasure.

3 Incorporating Different Rhythms and Pressures

riation in rhythms and pressures can significantly enhance pleasure and arousal during xual encounters. In this chapter, we'll explore how to incorporate different rhythms and essures into various sexual activities to create a more enjoyable and satisfying experience r both partners.

nderstanding Rhythms and Pressures

ıythm refers to the pattern or tempo of movements, while pressure refers to the amount force applied during stimulation.

corporating variations in rhythm and pressure can stimulate different nerve endings, tensify sensations, and increase arousal.

echniques for Varying Rhythms

periment with different rhythms during manual stimulation, oral sex, and penetrative tercourse.

y alternating between slow and steady movements, rapid and fluttering motions, or a ombination of both to create varied sensations.

y attention to your partner's responses and adjust your rhythm based on their level of ousal and pleasure.

echniques for Varying Pressures

djusting pressure during stimulation can provide different levels of sensation and intensity.

art with light, teasing touches to build anticipation and gradually increase pressure as esired.

periment with firm pressure, gentle caresses, and everything in between to find what els most pleasurable for you and your partner.

Clitoral Stimulation

Vary pressure and rhythm when stimulating the clitoris with fingers, tongue, or sex toys.

Experiment with light, feathery touches, followed by firmer pressure and faster rhythms create waves of pleasure.

Communicate with your partner to determine the level of pressure and rhythm that feels most pleasurable.

G-spot Stimulation

When stimulating the G-spot manually or with a toy, experiment with different pressures and rhythms.

Try applying firm, consistent pressure to the front wall of the vagina with a "come hither" motion, varying the speed and intensity as desired.

Pay attention to your partner's responses to gauge what feels most pleasurable and adjust your technique accordingly.

Penetrative Intercourse

Varying rhythms and pressures during penetrative intercourse can enhance pleasure for both partners.

Experiment with different thrusting patterns, speeds, and depths to stimulate different areas of the vagina and increase arousal.

Incorporate pauses, changes in direction, and variations in pressure to create a more dynamic and pleasurable experience.

Communication and Feedback

Encourage open communication with your partner about what feels pleasurable and what doesn't during sexual activities.

Pay attention to your partner's verbal and non-verbal cues to gauge their level of arousal and adjust your rhythm and pressure accordingly.

Provide positive reinforcement for techniques or movements that feel good, and be receptive to feedback and guidance from your partner.

Chapter 6: Positions for Maximum Pleasure

6.1 Overview of Sex Positions for Optimal Stimulation of Women

Choosing the right sex position can greatly enhance stimulation and pleasure for women during intercourse. In this chapter, we'll explore a variety of sex positions that are known to provide optimal stimulation for women, helping to maximize pleasure and intimacy in the bedroom.

Missionary Position

The missionary position is a classic and versatile option that allows for deep penetration and intimate contact.

Women can control the angle of penetration by adjusting the position of their legs, allowing for increased stimulation of the G-spot and clitoris.

Cowgirl Position

In the cowgirl position, the woman straddles her partner and can control the depth, angle, and rhythm of penetration.

This position provides direct stimulation to the clitoris, allowing for greater control over the intensity of pleasure.

Doggy Style Position

The doggy style position offers deep penetration and allows for stimulation of the G-spot and A-spot (anterior fornix erogenous zone).

Women may find this position particularly pleasurable due to the angle of penetration and the potential for simultaneous clitoral stimulation.

Spooning Position

Spooning allows for intimate contact and deep penetration while providing a comfortable and relaxed experience.

This position can stimulate the G-spot and allow for easy access to the clitoris for manual stimulation.

Modified Missionary Position

In the modified missionary position, the woman elevates her legs, either by placing them on her partner's shoulders or holding them up.

This angle allows for deeper penetration and increased stimulation of the G-spot and A-spot.

Seated Position

The seated position allows for face-to-face intimacy and eye contact while providing stimulation of the clitoris and G-spot.

Women can control the angle and depth of penetration by adjusting their position and the position of their partner.

Standing Position

Standing positions, such as the standing doggy style or the standing missionary, offer a sense of novelty and excitement while providing deep penetration.

These positions can stimulate the G-spot and allow for manual stimulation of the clitoris.

Edge of the Bed Position

The edge of the bed position allows for comfortable support and deep penetration, with the woman lying on her back and her partner standing or kneeling.

This position offers easy access to the clitoris for manual stimulation and can stimulate the G-spot.

Reverse Cowgirl Position

In the reverse cowgirl position, the woman faces away from her partner and can control the depth, angle, and rhythm of penetration.

This position provides stimulation to the G-spot and A-spot while allowing for increased clitoral stimulation.

Oral Sex Positions

Various oral sex positions, such as the 69 position or the woman-on-top position, allow for direct stimulation of the clitoris and provide opportunities for mutual pleasure and intimacy.

6.2 Tips for Finding the Right Angles and Depths

Finding the right angles and depths during sexual activity can greatly enhance pleasure and satisfaction for both partners. In this chapter, we'll explore tips and techniques for discovering the optimal angles and depths for stimulation during various sexual activities.

Communication and Exploration

Encourage open communication with your partner about what feels pleasurable and what doesn't during sexual activity.

Explore different angles and depths together, experimenting with various positions and movements to find what works best for both of you.

Experiment with Different Positions

Try a variety of sex positions to discover which angles and depths provide the most stimulation and pleasure.

Explore positions that allow for deep penetration, such as missionary or doggy style, as well as positions that provide direct clitoral stimulation, such as cowgirl or spooning.

Adjust Your Positioning

Experiment with subtle adjustments to your positioning to change the angle and depth of penetration.

For example, try tilting your hips or adjusting the angle of your legs to target different areas inside the vagina and enhance stimulation.

Use Props or Pillows

Incorporate props or pillows to support your body and adjust the angle of penetration during sexual activity.

Elevating the hips with a pillow or cushion can change the angle of penetration and allow for deeper or more targeted stimulation.

Listen to Your Partner's Feedback

Pay attention to your partner's verbal and non-verbal cues to gauge their level of arousal and satisfaction.

Adjust your positioning and technique based on their feedback to ensure a pleasurable and enjoyable experience for both partners.

Try Different Depths of Penetration

Experiment with different depths of penetration to find what feels most pleasurable for both partners.

Vary the depth of penetration by adjusting the angle of your body or the position of your partner's hips.

Incorporate Manual Stimulation

Use your hands or fingers to provide additional stimulation to erogenous zones, such as the clitoris or G-spot, during penetrative intercourse.

Experiment with different techniques and pressures to enhance pleasure and arousal.

Take Your Time and Explore

Don't rush through sexual activity – take your time to explore and discover what feels best for both you and your partner.

Enjoy the process of experimenting with different angles and depths, and prioritize pleasure and intimacy in your sexual encounters.

6.3 Incorporating Variety and Experimentation into Your Sex Life

Variety and experimentation are essential elements of a healthy and fulfilling sex life. In this chapter, we'll explore the importance of incorporating variety into your sexual experiences and provide tips for experimenting with new activities, techniques, and fantasies.

Understanding the Importance of Variety

Variety can prevent sexual routine and boredom, keeping the spark alive in your relationship.

rying new things can enhance intimacy, communication, and trust between partners.

Incorporating variety into your sex life can lead to increased arousal, pleasure, and satisfaction for both partners.

Communicate Your Desires and Fantasies

Share your desires, fantasies, and interests with your partner in an open and non-judgmental way.

Encourage your partner to do the same, and explore ways to incorporate each other's fantasies into your sexual experiences.

Experiment with Different Activities

Try new sexual activities or techniques that you and your partner are curious about.

Experiment with different positions, role-playing scenarios, or types of stimulation to discover what excites and satisfies both of you.

Explore Sensory Stimulation

Incorporate sensory stimulation into your sex life by experimenting with different textures, temperatures, and sensations.

Use props such as feathers, ice cubes, or blindfolds to enhance arousal and pleasure.

Introduce Sex Toys

Experiment with incorporating sex toys into your sexual encounters to add variety and excitement.

Choose toys that appeal to both partners and explore different ways to use them for stimulation and pleasure.

Role-Playing and Fantasy Exploration

Explore role-playing scenarios and fantasies with your partner to add excitement and novelty to your sex life.

Discuss your fantasies beforehand and establish boundaries and consent to ensure a comfortable and enjoyable experience for both partners.

Try New Locations

Step outside of the bedroom and experiment with having sex in different locations, such a the kitchen, bathroom, or outdoors.

Exploring new environments can add excitement and spontaneity to your sexual encounters.

Incorporate Erotic Literature or Films

Read erotic literature or watch erotic films together to spark arousal and inspiration.

Use these resources as a jumping-off point for discussing new ideas and fantasies to explo together.

Take Turns Planning

Take turns planning sexual encounters or surprises for each other to keep things fresh and exciting.

Plan date nights or weekend getaways focused on exploring new sexual experiences and connecting with each other on a deeper level.

Be Open-Minded and Flexible

Approach experimentation with an open mind and a spirit of curiosity and adventure.

Be willing to try new things and explore new sensations, even if they're outside of your comfort zone.

Chapter 7: The Role of Sensory Stimulation

7.1 Incorporating Sensory Play into Sexual Experiences

Sensory play can add excitement, anticipation, and heightened arousal to sexual encounters. In this chapter, we'll explore the benefits of sensory play and provide tips for incorporating sensory elements into your sexual experiences.

Understanding Sensory Play

Sensory play involves engaging one or more of the five senses – sight, sound, taste, touch, and smell – to enhance arousal and pleasure during sexual activity.

Sensory stimulation can intensify sensations, increase anticipation, and create a deeper sense of connection between partners.

Benefits of Sensory Play

Sensory play can add novelty and excitement to your sex life, keeping things fresh and stimulating.

Engaging the senses can heighten arousal and pleasure, leading to more intense and satisfying orgasms.

Sensory play encourages exploration, communication, and creativity in the bedroom, strengthening intimacy between partners.

Tips for Incorporating Sensory Play

Experiment with different sensory elements to discover what excites and arouses you and your partner.

Start with gentle and non-threatening sensations, gradually increasing intensity as desired.

Communicate openly with your partner about your preferences, boundaries, and fantasies regarding sensory play.

Sensory Elements to Explore

Sight: Use blindfolds or dim lighting to enhance anticipation and focus on other senses.

Sound: Play music, use whispering or dirty talk, or incorporate erotic sounds to create ambiance and arousal.

Taste: Experiment with incorporating food items such as chocolate, whipped cream, or fruit into foreplay or oral sex.

Touch: Use feathers, silk scarves, or massage oils to stimulate the skin and heighten sensation.

Smell: Use scented candles, essential oils, or perfumes to create an inviting and arousing atmosphere.

Sensory-Focused Activities

Sensory massage: Use massage oils or lotions with different textures and scents to stimulate the senses and relax the body.

Sensory deprivation: Use blindfolds or earmuffs to temporarily remove one sense, intensifying sensations in other areas.

Sensory exploration: Take turns exploring each other's bodies with different sensory stimuli, such as ice cubes, feathers, or silk scarves.

Sensory Play during Oral Sex

Experiment with incorporating sensory elements into oral sex, such as using flavored lubricants or ice cubes to stimulate the genitals.

Use your breath, tongue, and lips to create varied sensations and intensify pleasure.

Incorporating Sensory Play into Role-Playing

Use sensory elements to enhance role-playing scenarios, such as incorporating blindfolds or restraints for added excitement and anticipation.

Explore fantasies that involve sensory deprivation or heightened sensory experiences.

7.2 Using Props, Toys, and Accessories to Enhance Pleasure

Props, toys, and accessories can add excitement, novelty, and enhanced sensation to sexual encounters. In this chapter, we'll explore the benefits of incorporating these items into your sex life and provide tips for selecting and using them to enhance pleasure.

Benefits of Props, Toys, and Accessories

Props, toys, and accessories can add variety and novelty to your sexual experiences, keeping things fresh and exciting.

They can help stimulate erogenous zones, enhance arousal, and intensify orgasms for both partners.

Incorporating props and toys into your sex life can encourage exploration, communication, and creativity in the bedroom, deepening intimacy between partners.

Tips for Selecting Props, Toys, and Accessories

Consider your interests, preferences, and comfort level when selecting props, toys, and accessories.

Start with items that appeal to both you and your partner and explore different options together.

Prioritize safety and quality when selecting props and toys, choosing body-safe materials and reputable brands.

Types of Props, Toys, and Accessories to Explore

Sensory props: Incorporate items such as feathers, silk scarves, massage oils, or scented candles to stimulate the senses and enhance arousal.

Sex toys: Experiment with vibrators, dildos, anal toys, or other sex toys designed for solo or partnered use to add variety and intensity to your sexual encounters.

Restraints and bondage gear: Explore restraints, blindfolds, cuffs, or other bondage gear to introduce power dynamics and sensory deprivation into your play.

Role-playing costumes and accessories: Dress up in costumes, lingerie, or role-playing outfits to explore different fantasies and scenarios with your partner.

How to Incorporate Props, Toys, and Accessories into Your Play

Communicate openly with your partner about your interests, fantasies, and boundaries regarding the use of props, toys, and accessories.

Start by introducing props or toys during foreplay to enhance arousal and build anticipation.

Experiment with different ways to incorporate props and toys into your sexual encounters, such as using them during oral sex, penetrative intercourse, or role-playing scenarios.

Take turns exploring each other's bodies with props and toys, focusing on different erogenous zones and sensations.

7.3 Exploring the Connection between Sensory Stimulation and Arousal

Sensory stimulation plays a vital role in arousal, enhancing pleasure, and deepening intimacy between partners. In this chapter, we'll delve into the connection between sensory stimulation and arousal, exploring how engaging the senses can heighten sexual excitement and satisfaction.

Understanding Sensory Stimulation

Sensory stimulation involves engaging one or more of the five senses: sight, sound, taste, touch, and smell.

Engaging the senses during sexual activity can intensify sensations, increase arousal, and create a deeper sense of connection between partners.

Heightened Sensation and Arousal

Sensory stimulation activates nerve endings throughout the body, sending signals to the brain that trigger arousal and pleasure responses.

Stimulating the senses can lead to increased blood flow, heightened sensitivity, and heightened sexual arousal.

Enhancing Sensory Stimulation for Arousal

Sight: Dimming the lights, using candles, or incorporating erotic visuals can enhance visual stimulation and arousal.

Sound: Playing music, using erotic sounds, or engaging in dirty talk can heighten auditory stimulation and arousal.

Taste: Incorporating food items such as chocolate, whipped cream, or fruit into foreplay or oral sex can enhance taste sensation and arousal.

ouch: Using feathers, silk scarves, massage oils, or varying pressures and textures can imulate the skin and increase tactile arousal.

mell: Using scented candles, essential oils, or perfumes can create an inviting and arousing mosphere, enhancing olfactory stimulation.

Multi-Sensory Stimulation

ngaging multiple senses simultaneously can amplify arousal and pleasure during sexual ctivity.

xperiment with combining sensory elements, such as using scented candles while playing oft music, to create a multi-sensory experience.

uilding Anticipation and Excitement

ensory stimulation can help build anticipation and excitement, heightening arousal levels efore sexual activity even begins.

corporate sensory elements into foreplay to tease and tantalize your partner, increasing nticipation and desire.

eepening Intimacy and Connection

ngaging in sensory exploration with your partner can deepen intimacy and strengthen the motional connection between you.

ommunicate openly about your desires, preferences, and boundaries regarding sensory imulation, fostering trust and understanding.

Mindfulness and Presence

eing mindful and present during sensory stimulation can enhance the intensity of arousal nd pleasure.

ocus on each sensation as it arises, allowing yourself to fully experience the pleasure and onnection of the moment.

Chapter 8: Emotional Connection and Intimacy

8.1 Importance of Emotional Connection in Sexual Pleasure

Emotional connection plays a crucial role in sexual pleasure, enhancing intimacy, satisfaction, and overall well-being for both partners. In this chapter, we'll explore the significance of emotional connection in sexual experiences and how it contributes to a fulfilling and deeply satisfying sex life.

Understanding Emotional Connection

Emotional connection refers to the bond, trust, and mutual understanding between partners, built on feelings of love, affection, and respect.

Emotional connection forms the foundation of a healthy and fulfilling relationship, influencing all aspects of intimacy, including sexual pleasure.

Enhancing Intimacy and Trust

Emotional connection fosters a sense of closeness and vulnerability between partners, allowing them to open up and express their desires, fantasies, and boundaries.

Trust and emotional intimacy create a safe and secure environment for exploring new sexual experiences and expressing vulnerability without fear of judgment.

Heightening Sensual Awareness

Emotional connection enhances sensual awareness, allowing partners to attune to each other's desires, preferences, and needs.

Partners who are emotionally connected are more adept at reading each other's cues and responding sensitively to changes in mood, arousal, and comfort levels.

Deepening Physical Pleasure

Emotional connection enhances physical pleasure by intensifying sensations and amplifyin arousal during sexual activity.

Feeling emotionally connected to your partner can heighten sensitivity to touch, increase pleasure, and lead to more satisfying orgasms.

Strengthening Communication and Intimacy

Emotional connection facilitates open and honest communication about sexual desires, fantasies, and boundaries.

Partners who feel emotionally connected are more likely to communicate openly, listen empathetically, and express appreciation for each other's needs and desires.

Fostering Mutual Satisfaction

Emotional connection promotes mutual satisfaction and fulfillment in sexual experiences, prioritizing both partners' pleasure and well-being.

When partners are emotionally connected, they are more invested in each other's pleasure and derive satisfaction from their partner's enjoyment.

Creating Lasting Bonds

Emotional connection deepens over time through shared experiences, mutual support, and ongoing communication.

Cultivating emotional connection in your relationship strengthens the bond between partners and creates a solid foundation for long-term sexual fulfillment and relationship satisfaction.

8.2 Building Intimacy Through Communication and Trust

Communication and trust are foundational elements in building intimacy and fostering a deeply satisfying and fulfilling relationship. In this chapter, we'll explore the importance of communication and trust in nurturing intimacy, both inside and outside the bedroom, and provide strategies for strengthening these vital aspects of your relationship.

22.1 Understanding the Role of Communication

Communication involves expressing thoughts, feelings, desires, and needs openly and honestly with your partner.

Effective communication fosters understanding, empathy, and connection, strengthening the bond between partners.

22.2 Establishing Trust

Trust is the foundation of a healthy and secure relationship, built on honesty, reliability, and mutual respect.

Trusting your partner creates a safe and supportive environment for vulnerability and emotional intimacy.

22.3 Benefits of Communication and Trust in Building Intimacy

Communication and trust form the basis of emotional connection and intimacy, fostering a deep sense of closeness and understanding between partners.

Open communication and trust create a safe space for expressing desires, fantasies, and boundaries, enhancing sexual satisfaction and pleasure.

Strategies for Building Communication and Trust

Practice active listening: Listen attentively to your partner without interrupting or judging, and reflect back what you hear to ensure understanding.

Be honest and transparent: Share your thoughts, feelings, and experiences openly and authentically with your partner, even when it feels uncomfortable.

Express appreciation and validation: Acknowledge and appreciate your partner's efforts, strengths, and contributions to the relationship, reinforcing feelings of love and connection.

Foster empathy and understanding: Put yourself in your partner's shoes, empathize with their experiences and emotions, and validate their feelings, even if you don't always agree.

Prioritize quality time together: Carve out dedicated time to connect with your partner, engage in meaningful conversations, and share experiences that strengthen your bond.

Be reliable and consistent: Follow through on your commitments, be dependable, and demonstrate reliability to build trust and security in your relationship.

8.3 Techniques for Deepening Emotional Connection During Sex

Sexual intimacy provides a unique opportunity to deepen emotional connection and strengthen the bond between partners. In this chapter, we'll explore techniques and strategies for fostering emotional connection during sexual encounters, enhancing intimacy, satisfaction, and overall relationship fulfillment.

Prioritize Presence and Mindfulness

Practice being fully present and engaged during sexual activity, focusing on the sensations, emotions, and connection between you and your partner.

Cultivate mindfulness by tuning into your breath, bodily sensations, and the sensory experience of sex, deepening your connection with each moment.

Maintain Eye Contact

Eye contact during sex can foster intimacy and connection, allowing partners to communicate love, desire, and vulnerability without words.

Gaze into each other's eyes during moments of closeness and connection, deepening the emotional bond between you.

Communicate Verbally and Non-Verbally

Use verbal and non-verbal cues to express your desires, pleasure, and emotional connection during sex.

Whisper words of love, appreciation, and desire to your partner, and respond to their moans, sighs, and body language with sensitivity and attentiveness.

Engage in Sensual Touch

Use touch to convey love, affection, and desire to your partner, deepening emotional connection and arousal.

Explore sensual touch beyond erogenous zones, caressing each other's bodies with tenderness and reverence, fostering intimacy and connection.

Share Fantasies and Desires

Create a safe and non-judgmental space for sharing sexual fantasies, desires, and preferences with your partner.

Discuss your deepest desires, fantasies, and curiosities with openness and vulnerability, strengthening emotional connection and mutual understanding.

Practice Mutual Pleasure and Generosity

Prioritize mutual pleasure and satisfaction during sexual encounters, focusing on giving as well as receiving pleasure.

Take turns pleasuring each other, expressing generosity, and selflessness in your sexual interactions, deepening emotional connection and intimacy.

Engage in Aftercare

After sexual activity, engage in aftercare rituals to nurture emotional connection and provide comfort and reassurance to your partner.

Cuddle, hold each other, and engage in gentle touch or soothing words, reinforcing feelings of love, intimacy, and connection.

Printed in Great Britain
by Amazon

37550714R00030